Benefit-Cost Analysis in Environmental, Health, and Safety Regulation

Benefit-Cost Analysis in Environmental, Health, and Safety Regulation

A Statement of Principles

Kenneth J. Arrow,
Maureen L. Cropper,
George C. Eads, Robert W. Hahn,
Lester B. Lave, Roger G. Noll,
Paul R. Portney, Milton Russell,
Richard Schmalensee,
V. Kerry Smith, and
Robert N. Stavins

American Enterprise Institute,
The Annapolis Center, and
Resources for the Future

1996

This work was jointly sponsored by the American Enterprise Institute, the Annapolis Center, and Resources for the Future. Funding was provided by the Annapolis Center. We would like to thank Elizabeth Drembus and Jonathan Sisken for their editorial assistance and Richard Seibert, Meaghan Hayward, and Mary Moran for their administrative support. The views in this document represent those of the authors and do not necessarily represent the views of the institutions with which they are affiliated.

Distributed to the Trade by National Book Network, 15200 NBN Way, Blue Ridge Summit, PA 17214. To order call toll free 1-800-462-6420 or 1-717-794-3800. For all other inquiries please contact the AEI Press, 1150 Seventeenth Street, N.W., Washington, D.C. 20036 or call 1-800-862-5801.

ISBN 0-8447-7066-3

3 5 7 9 10 8 6 4 2

ISBN 978-0-8447-7066-6

Contents

Preface

The direct costs of federal environmental, health, and safety regulations are probably on the order of $200 billion annually, or about the size of all federal domestic, nondefense discretionary spending. The benefits of those regulations are even less certain. Evidence suggests that some recent regulations would pass a benefit-cost test while others would not.

The growing impact of regulations on the economy has led both Congress and the administration to search for new ways of reforming regulation. Many of those regulatory reform initiatives call for greater reliance on the use of economic analysis in the development and evaluation of regulations. Because ideological extremes have dominated debate on this topic, a dispassionate commentary may be particularly valuable.

On September 29, 1995, a group of leading economists met to discuss the role of economic analysis in the development of environmental, health, and safety regulation. The meeting was sponsored jointly by the American Enterprise Institute, the Annapolis Center, and Resources for the Future and was cochaired by Robert W. Hahn and Paul R. Portney. We would like to thank Harrison H. Schmitt, chairman of the Annapolis Center, for providing us with the resources necessary to undertake this endeavor. The following economists participated in the meeting:

Kenneth J. Arrow, *Stanford University*
Maureen L. Cropper, *World Bank*
George C. Eads, *Charles River Associates, Inc.*
Robert W. Hahn, *American Enterprise Institute*
Lester B. Lave, *Carnegie Mellon University*
Roger G. Noll, *Stanford University*
Paul R. Portney, *Resources for the Future*
Milton Russell, *University of Tennessee*
Richard Schmalensee, *Massachusetts Institute of Technology*
V. Kerry Smith, *Duke University*
Robert N. Stavins, *Harvard University*

The following report summarizes the key findings of our group. It consists of an executive summary along with a more detailed statement of the principles the group developed. The principles are divided into two sections. The first provides some guidance for decisionmakers on using economic analysis to evaluate laws and regulations. The second offers specific suggestions for improving the quality of economic analysis in regulatory decisionmaking. We hope that those findings will stimulate a reasoned discussion of the appropriate role of economic analysis in the development of regulations.

Benefit-Cost Analysis in Environmental, Health, and Safety Regulation

Executive Summary

Benefit-cost analysis can play a very important role in legislative and regulatory policy debates on improving the environment, health, and safety. It can help illustrate the tradeoffs that are inherent in public policymaking as well as make those tradeoffs more transparent. It can also help agencies set regulatory priorities.

Benefit-cost analysis should be used to help decisionmakers reach a decision. Contrary to the views of some, benefit-cost analysis is neither necessary nor sufficient for designing sensible public policy. If properly done, it can be very helpful to agencies in the decisionmaking process.

Decisionmakers should not be precluded from considering the economic benefits and costs of different policies in the development of regulations. Laws that prohibit costs or other factors from being considered in administrative decisionmaking are inimical to good public policy. Currently, several of the most important regulatory statutes have been interpreted to imply such prohibitions.

Benefit-cost analysis should be required for all major

regulatory decisions, but agency heads should not be bound by a strict benefit-cost test. Instead, they should be required to consider available benefit-cost analyses and to justify the reasons for their decision in the event that the expected costs of a regulation far exceed the expected benefits. Agencies should be encouraged to use economic analysis to help set regulatory priorities. Economic analyses prepared in support of particularly important decisions should be subjected to peer review both inside and outside government.

Benefits and costs of proposed major regulations should be quantified wherever possible. Best estimates should be presented along with a description of the uncertainties. Not all benefits or costs can be easily quantified, much less translated into dollar terms. Nevertheless, even qualitative descriptions of the pros and cons associated with a contemplated action can be helpful. Care should be taken to ensure that quantitative factors do not dominate important qualitative factors in decisionmaking.

The Office of Management and Budget, or some other coordinating agency, should establish guidelines that agencies should follow in conducting benefit-cost analyses. Those guidelines should specify default values for the discount rate and certain types of benefits and costs, such as the value of a small reduction in mortality risk. In addition, agencies should present their results using a standard format, which summarizes the key results and highlights major uncertainties.

Principles

Part One: Guidance for Decisionmakers on Using Economic Analysis to Evaluate Proposed Policies

Principle 1: *A benefit-cost analysis is a useful way of organizing a comparison of the favorable and unfavorable effects of proposed policies.*

Benefit-cost analysis can help the decisionmaker better understand the implications of a decision. It should be used to inform decisionmakers. Benefit-cost analysis can provide useful estimates of the overall benefits and costs of proposed policies. It can also assess the impacts of proposed policies on consumers, workers, and owners of firms and can identify potential winners and losers.

In many cases, benefit-cost analysis cannot be used to prove that the economic benefits of a decision will exceed or fall short of the costs. There is simply too much uncertainty in some of the estimates of benefits and costs to make such statements with a high degree of confidence.

Benefit-cost analysis should play an important role in informing the decisionmaking process, even when the information on benefits, costs, or both is highly uncertain, as is often the case with regulations involving the environment, health, and safety. The estimation of benefits and costs of a proposed regulation can provide illuminating evidence for a decision, even if precision cannot be achieved because of limitations on time, resources, or the availability of information.

Principle 2: *Economic analysis can be useful in designing regulatory strategies that achieve a desired goal at the lowest possible cost.*

Too frequently, environmental, health, and safety regulation has used a one-size-fits-all or command-and-control approach. Economic analysis can highlight the extent to which cost savings can be achieved by using alternative, more flexible approaches that reward performance. Performance standards and market-based approaches are generally preferable to command-and-control approaches because they can achieve the same objective at a lower total cost to society. A recent example is the market-based approach used to reduce emissions that cause acid rain. That approach was estimated to be much less expensive than an alternative under consideration that would have required large power plants to install scrubbers.

Principle 3: *Congress should not preclude decisionmakers from considering the economic benefits and costs of different policies in the development of regulations. At the very least, agencies should be encouraged to use economic analysis to help set regulatory priorities.*

Sections of some statutes, such as parts of the Clean Air Act and the Delaney Clause, explicitly prohibit the balancing of benefits and costs in the development of regulations. Removing such prohibitions can help promote more efficient and effective regulation of the environment, health, and safety.

To make better use of society's resources, Congress should encourage regulatory agencies to use economic analysis in planning their regulatory agenda. Current planning in most regulatory agencies places insufficient emphasis on the likely benefits and costs of regulations and excessive emphasis on politics and deadlines. Congress should consider changing that emphasis by explicitly asking agencies to consider the benefits and costs of policies in formulating agendas.

Principle 4: *Benefit-cost analysis should be required for all major regulatory decisions.*

While the precise definition of *major* requires some judgment, we believe that a major regulation should be one whose annual economic cost is expected to be greater than $100 million. We also believe that this requirement should be applied to independent agencies as well as to executive branch agencies. An important benefit of mandatory benefit-cost analysis is that it facilitates external monitoring of an agency's performance and thus makes it easier to hold agency heads accountable.

The scale of a benefit-cost analysis should depend on both the stakes involved and the likelihood that the resulting information will affect the ultimate decision. Other things equal, agencies should devote more resources to analyzing problems where the stakes are greater. A full-blown benefit-cost analysis, however, can be costly. Therefore, the agency should not perform the analysis unless there is some likelihood that doing so will actually inform the regulatory decision. Informing the decision could involve changing the goal of the regulation or the means by which a particular goal is achieved.

Principle 5: *Agencies should not be bound by a strict benefit-cost test, but should be required to consider available benefit-cost analyses. For regulations whose expected costs far exceed expected benefits, agency heads should be required to present a clear explanation justifying the reasons for their decision.*

There may be factors other than economic benefits and costs that agencies will want to weigh in decisions, such as equity within and across generations. In addition, a decisionmaker may want to place greater weight on particular characteristics of a decision, such as potential irreversible consequences.

Principle 6: *For legislative proposals involving major health, safety, and environmental regulations, the Congressional Budget Office should do a preliminary benefit-cost analysis that can inform legislative decisionmaking.*

Because laws give rise to regulations, some kind of benefit-cost analysis is likely to be useful in informing the policy process. Such a benefit-cost analysis will, of necessity, be quite rough since it is difficult to estimate the economic impact of a proposed law before the regulations based on that law are written. Although a full-blown benefit-cost analysis may not be warranted in many cases, a rough benefit-cost analysis will often be quite useful.

Part Two: Suggestions for Improving the Quality of Economic Analysis Used in Regulatory Decisionmaking

Principle 7: *While benefit-cost analysis should focus primarily on the overall relationship between benefits and costs, a good benefit-cost analysis will identify important distributional consequences of a policy.*

Available data often permit reliable estimation of major policy impacts on important subgroups of the population. If a regulation results in economic spillovers that contribute to significant job losses or increased costs to a specific industry in a local economy, then it is appropriate to consider those in a benefit-cost analysis. Agencies should, however, weigh those impacts against positive impacts that result elsewhere in the larger economy. Usually, it is better to address concerns about local economic spillover effects of regulation by using tax and transfer policies rather than regulatory policy.

Regulation typically affects the distribution of employment among industries rather than the general employment level. Usually, any specific regulation has a very minor effect on either wages or employment in the industry to which it applies. Regardless of the size of the employment effect, the appropriate measure of regulatory costs is the transition costs of employees who are forced to switch jobs because of the regulation. In those few cases where regulation can have a significant impact on total employment, such as the minimum wage, the effect on consumers and producers should also be estimated.

Principle 8: *It is important to identify the incremental benefits and costs associated with different regulatory policies.*

A problem with many regulatory analyses is that they fail to specify a clear baseline. Doing so is a necessary first step in identifying the incremental benefits and costs of a proposed policy. Defining a clear baseline can help avoid problems with double counting. For example, some regulatory analyses have counted as benefits positive changes that would have occurred even if the regulations were not implemented.

In addition to specifying a clear baseline, we think it is useful for the analyst to consider an array of practical alternatives for pursuing a particular statutory or regulatory objective, while carefully noting the incremental benefits and costs associated with those alternatives. For example, almost all of the harm from a polluting process can frequently be eliminated for a reasonable cost, while an astronomical cost is required to remove the last, small amount of harm. A benefit-cost analysis that considers only a no-treatment baseline and a full-treatment alternative may find that benefits exceed the costs under full treatment. If the analysis had considered a partial-treatment case, however, the net benefits to consumers could be higher still. In that example, separate consideration of low-cost and high-cost alternatives makes it easier for the decisionmaker to select the low-cost remedy when it is appropriate.

Principle 9: *Benefits and costs of proposed policies should be quantified wherever possible. Best estimates should be presented along with a description of the uncertainties.*

In most instances, it should be possible to describe the effects of proposed policy changes in quantitative terms. Quantification of benefits and costs is useful, even where there are large uncertainties. Available methods and data generally imply ranges of possible values of benefits and costs, not single numbers. Benefit-cost analysis contributes most to intelligent decisionmaking when those ranges are clearly described along with best estimates. Best estimates should reflect expected values.

If the decisionmaker wishes to introduce a "margin of safety" into his decision, he should do so explicitly. Assumptions should be stated clearly rather than be hidden within the analysis.

Principle 10: *Not all impacts of a decision can be quantified or expressed in dollar terms. Care should be taken to ensure that quantitative factors do not dominate important qualitative factors in decisionmaking.*

A common critique of benefit-cost analysis is that it does not emphasize factors that are not easily quantified or monetized. That critique has merit. There are two principal ways to address it: first, quantify as many factors as are reasonable and quantify or characterize the relevant uncertainties; and second, give due consideration to factors that defy quantification but are thought to be important.

Principle 11: *The more external review regulatory analyses receive, the better they are likely to be.*

External review includes peer-reviewed studies as well as studies reviewed by an agency other than the one doing the study. Historically, the Office of Management and Budget has played a key role in reviewing selected major regulations, particularly those aimed at protecting the environment, health, and safety. We think that such a role is appropriate for any regulation whose annual economic cost is expected to be greater than $100 million.

Peer review of economic analyses should be used for regulations with potentially large economic impacts (for example, those whose annual economic cost exceeds $1 billion). The reviewers should be selected on the basis of their demonstrated expertise and reputation.

Retrospective assessments of selected regulatory impact analyses should also be done periodically by an independent group of scholars to address systematic problems that have arisen. Because environmental, health, and safety regulatory decisions can have important impacts on the economy, it is useful to review periodically the quality of economic analysis that aids in the decisionmaking process. An outside panel of experts, primarily consisting of economists and other scientists, could provide recommendations on how such analyses could be improved. The panel could be selected by the National Academy of Sciences.

Principle 12: *A core set of economic assumptions should be used in calculating benefits and costs associated with environmental, health, and safety regulation. Key variables include the social discount rate, the value of reducing risks of dying and accidents, and the value associated with other improvements in health.*

There are benefits from being able to compare results across analyses, including potentially large gains in economic efficiency. A common set of economic assumptions facilitates such comparisons. For example, a common set of assumptions can be used to develop values for improvements in environmental quality.

Agencies should be allowed to use alternative assumptions, so long as those assumptions are clearly stated. They should then compare the results based on those assumptions with the results based on the common set of assumptions. Where possible, agencies should explain the economic rationale for employing alternative assumptions.

Principle 13: *Information should be presented clearly and succinctly in a regulatory impact analysis. Transparency is necessary if benefit-cost analysis is to inform decisionmaking.*

It is very important in conducting a benefit-cost analysis that agencies spell out all key assumptions clearly and highlight uncertainties. Both the executive summary and the report itself should be easily accessible to people who are familiar with basic economic concepts. References for key estimates should be provided.

The executive summary of the analysis should present key assumptions and results for the base case and sensitivity analyses. That summary should include information on the net present value of benefits and costs and the stream of benefits and costs for all cases that the analysis examines in detail. It should also highlight key factors that have been quantified as well as those that have not. Finally, the summary should identify incremental net benefits from selecting different alternatives.

Principle 14: *A single agency should set key economic values for evaluating regulations and should develop a standard format for presenting the results of a regulatory impact analysis.*

A single agency, such as the Office of Management and Budget, should specify key economic values for use in evaluating proposed regulations. That approach will ensure that there is some consistency across agency evaluations. Those values should be revised periodically on the basis of new information.

A single agency, such as the Office of Management and Budget, should also develop a standard format for presenting key assumptions and results. That format should make it easier for decisionmakers and interested parties to review principal findings.

Principle 15: *Whenever possible, values used for monetizing benefits and costs should be based on tradeoffs that individuals would make, either directly or, as is often the case, indirectly in labor, housing, or other markets.*

Benefit-cost analysis is premised on the notion that the values to be assigned to program effects—favorable or unfavorable—are those of the affected individuals, not the values held by economists, moral philosophers, or others. Valuation will be difficult, and in some cases impossible, when individuals are unwilling or unable to substitute one commodity or service for another.

Because one seldom knows whose life will be prolonged or whose health will be improved by a regulatory program, it is generally appropriate to value small reductions in the risk of morbidity or premature mortality for each individual. Typically, individuals are willing to trade off other amenities, goods, or services for slight reductions in risk. The values they reveal depend on both the type of risk and the number of additional years of life they would enjoy from reduced risk. Other things being equal, a program that prevents a serious illness should be valued more highly than one that prevents a minor ailment. Similarly, a program that extends a life by thirty years should be valued more highly than one that extends it for three years. Where policies are expected to extend a life, it is better to estimate the number of life-years extended than just the number of lives.

Principle 16: *Given uncertainties in identifying the correct discount rate, it is appropriate to employ a range of rates. Ideally, the* *same range of discount rates should be used in all regulatory analyses.*

Both economic efficiency and intergenerational equity require that benefits and costs experienced in future years be given less weight in decisionmaking than those experienced today. The rate at which future benefits and costs should be discounted to present values will generally not equal the rate of return on private investment. The discount rate should instead be based on how individuals trade off current for future consumption.

About the Authors

Kenneth J. Arrow is the Joan Kenney Professor of Economics Emeritus at Stanford University. His research interests include foundations and applications of welfare criteria, general equilibrium analysis, and the economics of uncertainty and information. He has received the Nobel Memorial Prize in Economic Science, the John Bates Clark Medal, and the von Neumann Prize. He has also been president of several learned societies.

Maureen L. Cropper is a principal economist at the World Bank, a professor of economics at the University of Maryland, and a senior fellow at Resources for the Future. Her research has focused on valuing environmental amenities—especially environmental health effects—from both an empirical and a theoretical perspective. She has also completed studies of the U.S. Environmental Protection Agency's decisionmaking that infer the value of lives saved by various regulations, as well as the implicit value of Superfund cleanup options. Her current research centers on valuing the health impacts of pollution in developing countries and on the economics of deforestation.

George C. Eads is a vice president for Charles River Associates, Inc. Before joining Charles River's Washington office, he was a vice president of General Motors and the corporation's chief economist. Mr. Eads was a member of President Carter's Council of Economic Advisers and oversaw the CEA's regulatory reform activities and chaired the Carter administration's interagency Regulatory Analysis Review Group. In the mid-1970s he was the first assistant director for the Council on Wage and Price Stability and initiated that agency's policy of filing written comments on the economic impact of major proposed federal rules and regulations.

Robert W. Hahn is a resident scholar at the American Enterprise Institute, a research associate at Harvard University, and an adjunct professor of economics at Carnegie Mellon University. Before that he worked for two years as a senior staff member of the President's Council of Economic Advisers. Mr. Hahn frequently contributes to general-interest periodicals and leading scholarly journals including the *New York Times*, the *Wall Street Journal*, the *American Economic Review*, and the *Yale Law Journal*. In addition, he is a cofounder of the Community Preparatory School—an inner-city middle school that provides opportunities for disadvantaged youth to achieve their full potential. Mr. Hahn's current research interests include the reform of regulation in developed and developing countries and the design of new institutions for reforming regulation.

Lester B. Lave is University Professor and the Higgins Professor of Economics in the Graduate School of Industrial Administration and professor of engineering and public policy in the College of Engineering and Public Policy at Carnegie Mellon University. He has consulted to the U.S. Environmental Protection Agency, the Occupational Safety and Health Administration, and other federal government agencies on the theory and application of benefit-cost analysis. His current assignment as head of the Carnegie Mellon University-wide Green Design Initiative has resulted in analyses of electric cars, municipal solid waste recycling, and the weighting of toxic discharges that give practical demonstration to the controversies inherent in benefit-cost analysis.

Roger G. Noll is the Morris M. Doyle Professor of Public Policy in the Department of Economics at Stanford University. At Stanford, he is also the director of the Public Policy Program, the director of the Program in Regulatory Policy in the Center for Economic Policy Research, and a professor by courtesy in the Graduate School of Business and the Department of Political Science. Professor Noll's research interests include government regulation of business and public policies regarding research and development. Currently, he is evaluating the role of federalism in regulatory policy and is conducting international comparative studies of the performance of regulatory institutions and infrastructural industries.

Paul R. Portney is president of Resources for the Future. From 1989 to 1995, he was RFF's vice president and was the director of its Center for Risk Management and its Quality of the Environment Division. Before joining RFF, Mr. Portney was chief economist at the Council on Environmental Quality in the Executive Office of the President. He is currently a member of the Executive Committee of EPA's Science Advisory Board and chairman of the SAB's Environmental Economics Advisory Committee. He lectures frequently on developments in U.S. and international environmental policy. His most recent publication is *Footing the Bill for Superfund Cleanups: Who Pays and How?*

Milton Russell is professor of economics at the University of Tennessee, Knoxville, the director of the Joint Institute for Energy and Environment, and a collaborating scientist at Oak Ridge National Laboratory. He was an assistant administrator of the U.S. Environmental Protection Agency, a senior fellow at Resources for the Future, and a senior staff member of the Council of Economic Advisers. His research centers on environmental policy and decision-making, most recently as applied to hazardous waste remediation. He was elected a fellow of the Society of Risk Analysis in 1994.

Richard Schmalensee is the Gordon Y. Billard Professor of Economics and Management at the Massachusetts Institute of Technology and director of MIT's Center for Energy and Environmental Policy Research. He was a member of the President's Council of Economic Advisers from 1989 through 1991. Before joining the council, Professor Schmalensee was area head for economics, finance, and accounting at the MIT Sloan School of Management. His academic work has centered on industrial organization economics and its application to a wide range of antitrust and regulatory issues. Professor Schmalensee is a member of the U.S. Environmental Protection Agency's Environmental Economic Advisory Board and is chairman of its Clean Air Act Compliance Analysis Council.

V. Kerry Smith is the Arts and Sciences Professor of Environmental Economics at Duke University and a university fellow for the Quality of the Environment Division at Resources for the Future. Professor Smith is a past president of the Southern Economic Association and the Association of Environmental and Resource Economists. His advisory and consulting activities have focused on natural resource damage assessment, evaluation of regulations for air and water quality, valuation of risk reductions from hazardous waste policies, and environmental costing. His current research centers on modeling how individuals deal with risks—such as radon, pesticide residues, and cholesterol—that differ in their temporal effects and prospects for mitigation.

Robert N. Stavins is professor of public policy and chairman of the Environment and Natural Resources Program at the John F. Kennedy School of Government at Harvard

University. He is a university fellow at Resources for the Future, a member of the Environmental Economics Advisory Committee of the U.S. Environmental Protection Agency's Science Advisory Board, a member of the Intergovernmental Panel on Climate Change, and a member of the Eco-Efficiency Task Force of the President's Council on Sustainable Development. Professor Stavins's current research includes analyses of the innovation of energy-efficient technologies, methods for valuing environmental amenities, the design and implementation of incentive-based approaches to environmental protection, and alternative strategies for mitigating global climate change.

CONSENSUS DOCUMENTS OF RELATED INTEREST

AN AGENDA FOR FEDERAL REGULATORY REFORM
Robert W. Crandall, Christopher DeMuth,
Robert W. Hahn, Robert E. Litan, Pietro S. Nivola,
and Paul R. Portney

IMPROVING REGULATORY ACCOUNTABILITY
Robert W. Hahn and Robert E. Litan

Published by the American Enterprise Institute for Public Policy Research and the Brookings Institution in 1997.